Financial FREEDOM

Finding What Works for You

ENDORSEMENTS

"You were able to quickly identify our financial strengths and weaknesses and get us on course. Thank you for your insight and coaching."

—Pat C.

"I just want to thank you for all that you've done for me and my family. Your advice and counsel has been so appreciated over the years. Your personal touch has made all the information so much more understandable."

—Velma C.

"Thank you for helping me out. I can be a tough one but you kept coming at me with kindness and concern. You have helped me out a lot. I just hope I can keep improving."

—Myra E.

"We want to thank you so much for all you have done for us this year. The knowledge and advice you have given us is priceless. We always look forward to talking with you."

—Tonya B.

"I just wanted to thank you for your willingness to assist us and having us benefit from your wonderful program. Thanks again for going above and beyond the call of duty."

—Lloyd T.

"I want to thank you for all your help. Your coaching has made a big difference in my life and my outlook on life. It just amazes me how much I have learned. I know I think differently now than before I took your course. I hope that you will continue to help others as you have helped me."

—Norm S.

"I was out of the country when the stock market took a free fall. Because of your advice, my investments were already prepared for that and I didn't worry in the least."

—Emily D.

"Thanks Greg. You have made our financial life functional and our marriage better. We will be able to achieve our dreams."

—Mary & Mike C.

"We want to thank you so much for all you have done for us this year. The knowledge and advice you have given us is priceless! We always look forward to talking with you. Thanks for sharing in our journey."

—Ed & Terri B.

"You have coached, encouraged and accompanied Peter and I on quite a journey so far. We are so thankful for your guidance and friendship. We look forward to being associated with you for many years to come. Please know that you are touching lives and making a difference in the world."

—Sherri & Peter E.

"I would like to take the time to tell you how much I appreciate your example in my life. I've seen your example of how to be a strong leader and your willingness to understand what people go through in their life. I just wanted to take this opportunity to let you know how much I respect you."

—Carrie L.

Financial FREEDOM

Finding What Works for You

GREG KESTEN

BookWise publishing

Financial Freedom: Finding What Works for You

Greg Kesten

The identities and situations of individuals in the stories contained in this book have been altered to protect individual privacy.

The intent of the author is only to offer information of a general nature to help you in your quest for financial well-being.

BookWise Publishing, Riverton, Utah

Library of Congress Control Number: 2014922398

Interior book design: Eden Graphics, Inc. www.edengraphics.net

ISBN: 978-1-60645-129-8

10 9 8 7 6 5 4 3 2 1

First Printing

PRINTED IN THE UNITED STATES OF AMERICA

TABLE OF CONTENTS

ACKNOWLEDGMENTS

Thomas Payne once said, "Writing is easy. You just get a blank piece of paper and bleed all over it." I never realized what really goes into writing a book, but I know now, and it is a huge endeavor. The tasks would not have been completed without the assistance, insight, and talent of many people.

I would like to thank my wife, Leslie, whose assistance is invaluable in editing my work and helping me in my practice. I don't know what I would do without her.

I would also like to recognize my three adult children; Chris, Scott and Lani. They have taught me so much over the years. It is enjoyable to watch them navigate through life with their families and their finances. To observe their financial stability has been a wonderful reminder that Leslie and I have done something right.

To my long time associate, Jeff Isaacson who started with me in this business over three decades ago. We have been through great learning experiences ever since.

I'm grateful to Karen Christoffersen for her professional insight that made this endeavor doable. Also, Crystal Liechty, Fran Platt, and Lowell Oswald for stepping up with their specific expertise and being so readily available to do their part. In surrounding myself with this amazing team, we have done amazing things.

My gratitude to my good friend, Dave Blanchard, for his absolute focus on helping people. He is a constant example of how great things come to pass when one is willing to serve and create value in others' lives.

Being financially secure, independent, and free is an important part of one's life, but it is not the most important part. I believe the most important parts of one's life are the events we experience when we feel blessed and at peace with the quality of our lives.

Although I have helped many people become millionaires, doing it in a systematic and measurable way, I have never lost sight of how much I love the people I've been able to serve. My clients come from all walks of life, and they all have one thing in common: they are great people who want to make a difference in the world and in the lives of their families and others. My clients have all come to me motivated with a desire to be better and do better. I feel very grateful they have allowed me to be part of their lives. This book is for anyone who is serious about their money and is ready to take their life to the next level.

FOREWORD

When Greg said there was a book inside of him that he always wanted to write, we all encouraged him to go for it. Great books are borne out of extensive down-in-the-trenches experience and thorough preparation. Greg did not have aspirations of writing a book that would make him rich and famous or help him sell products. He had a burning desire to share the time-tested financial principles that have served him and hundreds of his clients over the past thirty plus years as a well-respected financial coach. This is the first step in writing a great book—pure intent.

I vividly remember the Saturday morning I carved out time to read the first draft. Sitting in the leather reclining love seat in our master bedroom, a sacred place where Ramona and I have spent many hours reading together and talking about those things that matter most, it was time to open the first page. The setting was fitting for the experience that was about to unfold.

A couple of hours later, looking up while contemplating the words, I was pleased to discover how they were prompting several very personal impressions. Who would have expected such a profound experience from such a simple and short book?

I knew and practiced many of these principles, but somehow Greg managed to get in that little crack behind the scenes and tenderly and so gently touch on the painful ones. There I sat in my favorite seat reflecting on things I had been ignoring or avoiding and of course not wanting anyone to know.

If Greg had tried to preach, rebellion would probably have been my response. If he were condescending, his words might have been summarily dismissed and the principles obscured. But he did not preach nor was he condescending. The words did not invoke shame for all that was not perfect. Instead the words inspired action that would create needed change. This is a critical step in writing a great book.

I reached over and picked up the phone and dialed his number. It was important that the call be made right then while everything was so fresh. It was important that Greg know he'd done it—he'd written a great book. I wanted to share it with our children and grandchildren and promote it within the Og Mandino community. This is the best step in writing a great book—people want to share it with those they love the most.

It is vital that you read this book and have your

own experience. Even more important than the words you read will be the impressions that come. Read this book with a pen and paper by your side. Record your impressions and trust them. Commit to take the actions suggested. Make this decision and, in time, financial freedom will by yours.

Thank you, Greg, for having the courage to take this difficult subject head on. Clearly your vast experience and real-time example of how to live these financial principles found their way to the pages of this book and in a way that could serve everyone from every walk of life—from the wealthy to the deeply indebted.

—Dave Blanchard
CEO of The Og Mandino Group and author of
Today I Begin a New Life and *The Observer's Chair*

INTRODUCTION

Why I Do What I Do

We all learn about money from somewhere. Typically we spend our first 18,000 meals with the worst financial managers in the world, our parents. Their intentions were good, but their knowledge and practices were often lacking. Unfortunately, most people repeat the mistakes they are raised with or find themselves living the opposite extreme.

Although I spent my first 18,000 meals with sincere but poor financial managers, I didn't fully begin to understand the power of money until later—and in the most unexpected place.

More than four decades ago, I spent two years among the Polynesian people in the South Pacific islands of Samoa. I was a young man then, living 5,000 miles from home in a different culture, language and climate; among people who were completely different from anyone I'd ever met in my nineteen years growing up in California.

I learned a lot about money during those years; what money does—and what money doesn't do.

My companions and I lived with Samoan families on different islands. We'd often visit people during the day, getting to know them and seeking ways to be of service. We paid the families we stayed with six Samoan "tala" per week, or $10 USD, for the privilege of living in their home.

That $10 USD covered food, shelter, laundry, and any other related expenses. It turned out, I spent about $60 USD per month: $40 to the families I stayed with and $20 for other incidentals. I did this every month for two years. All totaled, I lived on about $1,440 for my entire two years in Samoa.

The most surprising thing is that living on $1,440 for that long was not only doable, it was comfortable and even enjoyable. The families I lived among spent even less. In 1973, an average Samoan family earned about $240 a year, or $20 a month—for the entire family.

So what did all this teach me about money?

- I learned that money is part of a process, not an outcome.

- I learned that a person can have a good life even if they only bring in what is sufficient for their needs.

- I learned that all you need is what you have for your life at that given time.

- I learned that money can be a benefit or a curse to the lives of people—depending on how it is used or shared.

- I learned that life is not about money, it's about having great relationships, good health, and sharing our time and talents with those around us.

I had many powerful, defining moments during my time in Samoa. I've realized every year since how much my belief system has been rooted in those experiences.

The difference between prosperity and poverty is our degree of gratitude. Once you realize that, you don't attach so much emotion to your money. A person bringing in $240 a year can find financial freedom while someone making far more can be far less free.

The definition of financial freedom is to have what you want and to want what you have. The first step is to know where you are financially.

The purpose of my book is to share with you this truth: *you can be financially free and live a great life.*

My Business Vision Statement

The purpose of my business is to improve the financial well-being and quality of life for my clients.

WORD	DEFINITION
Achievement	Something you've accomplished
Belief	A pattern of certainty in one's mind
Cash Flow	The amount of money you have coming in versus the amount of money you have going out
Coach	Someone who helps you achieve your objectives through knowledge, experience, teaching and support
Financial Freedom	Having what you want and wanting what you have
Financial Independence	When work is optional and leisure is affordable
Financial Security	Living within your means
Financial Vision	A positive, passionate description of your financial hopes, bringing them into the present
Goal	For something to be a goal, it should pass two tests: The measurement test: How much? By when? The acid test: Can I? (ability) Will I? (motivation)
Net Worth	Assets minus liabilities
Objectives	Planning for a prescribed outcome
Rich	Having a lot of money
Success	A *feeling* of accomplishment
Wealth	Being grateful for what you have

CHAPTER 1

Haves and Wants

All money is a matter of belief.

— Adam Smith —

The definition of **financial freedom** is: *what I have is what I want, and what I want is what I have.*

To be financially free, you need to line up two areas: the "haves" and the "wants." It's a powerful concept when you consider it. As long as you want something, you don't have it. So if you don't have what you want, you can't be free.

What's the difference between a have and a want?

A "have" is something we currently possess. A "want" is something we don't have at present, but desire. Those can be tangible items, like a certain kind of car or house; or intangible items, like love or fulfillment in your career choice.

You might be thinking, "Don't we always want to have more?"

Not necessarily.

For instance, if I just ate a big, five-course meal, how important is it for me to have another course? How many movies can you go to in a day? How many clothes can you fit in your closet? Every day, we have situations where we're totally satisfied with what we have.

Just because we live in a free society doesn't mean we always want or need to have more.

Ask yourself:

What would your quality of life be like if you had *exactly* what you wanted, and you wanted to have nothing more?

There are people who are satisfied having very little, compared to others. Think about people who live in seclusion or on self-sustaining farms. They have everything they want, as long as they have a roof over their heads, clothes on their backs and food to eat.

How much more do you need?

Always wanting more can become an addiction. This addiction keeps you constantly dissatisfied because you're always focused on what you don't have instead of what you do have. To want something is to lack that very thing.

What does it mean that "to want is to lack?"

When someone tells us they want something, they're automatically telling us that they're lacking. If I want a new car, that means I lack the car I want. But that doesn't mean I have no *car* or no *transportation options*.

As long as you're lacking, you're not free. A lot of what people lack are things they don't really need. A simple change in perspective would turn them from someone chained to various wants, to someone who is happy with what they have. Therefore they are financially free.

How to be free:

There is money you will never have, an amount of celebrity you'll never acquire, and a certain social status that you'll never achieve.

We, as individuals, can ask ourselves what we want to be free from. You may think that if you achieve something—fortune, fame, or status, for example—then that will give you the freedom to be who you want, or live how you want.

A study of the rich and famous will quickly reveal that fortune and fame seldom, if ever, equal happiness. Meanwhile, binding yourself to desires that you're unlikely to attain keeps you from happiness you could be enjoying right now, in this moment, by appreciating the things you already have.

There's a story told about a former Air Force pilot who visited a prison in California. He made a presentation to the inmates there about his service in the military during the Gulf War. After he spoke to this group of inmates, one of them came up to him and shook his hand.

The inmate said, "Thank you for keeping us free."

The veteran was surprised to hear someone who was locked behind prison bars express gratitude for freedom.

That inmate understood something many people lose sight of. He understood the value of living in a free country, even though he wasn't enjoying all those freedoms at the moment.

Financial freedom is about recognizing what you *have* rather than focusing on what you *want*.

Changing Your Perspective:

Think about the things you wish you had right now. Then answer the following questions honestly. List each specific desire. Go through all six questions for each specific "want" (for example: a promotion at work, new furniture, more savings, a better relationship with someone you love, etc.). See sample answers below.

1. What is something you want in your life right now?
2. Why do you want it?
3. What is keeping you from having it?
4. What are you willing to do to obtain it?
5. If you couldn't obtain it, what's the worst that could happen?
6. You might *want* it, but do you really need it?

Sample Answers:

1. What is something you want in your life right now?

A new car.

It's important to really identify the things you want. Sometimes there's just a vague sense of not having enough. If you can sit down and be specific, it becomes a lot easier to set objectives for getting what you want. Or, once it's on paper, you may decide it's not as important to you as you thought.

2. Why do you want it?

- *I love the smell of a new car.*
- *I love the compliments I get from family, friends, and associates.*
- *People are more apt to recognize my financial success.*

We're so inundated with media messaging in our culture that sometimes we simply absorb our desires from others. If you'd never seen that car commercial, would you want a new car right now? In addition, the drive to compete can sometimes lead us to confuse our wants with the wants of others. Just because your neighbor has a riding lawnmower doesn't mean you need one. And if you'd never seen him using it, you probably wouldn't want one right now. So as we look at our wants, it's important to decide if it's something we truly want for ourselves, or if it's something we want because someone else has it.

3. What is keeping you from having that?

- *My spouse doesn't want a new car.*
- *I don't want a monthly payment.*
- *I haven't saved enough money to pay cash for a new car.*

This question may seem relatively straight-forward and most times the answer will be "not enough money." But for intangible things, like a good relationship with a spouse, money won't get you what you want. Some other answers to this question might be: not enough time, too stressed to try, fear of failure or lack of confidence. Take the time and figure out your honest answer to this question (for example, you don't have enough money because you don't have the confidence to ask for that promotion), because you can't get what you want if you're unclear about why you don't already have it.

4. **What are you willing to do to obtain it?**
   - *Work extra hours.*
   - *Get a second job.*
   - *Forgo a vacation and use the money for the car.*

If you've determined that your "want" is genuine, and that the obstacle preventing you from getting it is surmountable, the question becomes: what are you willing to do? If the answer is "anything," then *you* are the only thing standing in your way. If you're answer is "I'm not really sure I want to sacrifice anything for it," that's okay. It just means you need to stop beating yourself up for not having it.

5. **If you couldn't obtain it, what's the worst that could happen?**
   - *I'll regret it.*
   - *Life goes on.*
   - *Nothing.*

The answer to this question could go one of two ways: on the one hand, the want could be really important. For instance, if your want is "a good relationship with my spouse," then the worst that could happen could be divorce.

You may start to notice a trend as you answer these questions. Either the "wants" will start to grow, and you'll realize how important it is that you change your life to get them, or you'll see how unimportant the "want" really is and start liberating yourself from the desire.

6. You might *want* it, but do you really need it?

- *It's important for my business image.*
- *I need reliable transportation.*
- *The tax breaks would be good.*

This is what all the other questions have been leading to. If you don't really *need* your "want," then it's time to let it go and re-orient yourself toward financial freedom and the ability to be happy with what you have.

If you discover that you really do need it, then you need to embrace that and do what it takes to make it happen.

Either way, facing your "wants" head on is an important step to achieving financial freedom.

I began working with Rick and Karen fifteen years ago. They live in New York and, although they're millionaires, they never feel like they have enough. They constantly express concern that they need more money in order to retire.

We revisit this conversation often. It's as if I have to re-teach and remind them in each of our sessions that they have plenty to retire on if they want to maintain their current lifestyle.

The fact is, most people do not want to retire in luxury; they want to retire with the same quality of life they currently enjoy.

I continue to work with Rick and Karen, helping them become wealthy—grateful for what they have, *and* rich—able to bring in plenty of money to support the lifestyle they desire.

The unfortunate thing is how quickly they forget the wealth and riches they already earned because, emotionally, they always want more—more money for travel, additional homes, newer cars, etc.

The "haves" and "wants" are the crux of financial freedom. Most millionaires I work with get trapped in the cycle of always wanting what is just out of reach.

I worked with Vivian and her husband for many years. I continued to work with Vivian after her husband passed away. One day, she called to ask for some advice. She wanted to know what she should do with an extra $200 a month she was saving.

"I thought your only income was social security," I said, remembering it was $1,400 a month. "Where are you coming up with an additional $200 for savings?"

"I only spend $1,200 a month, so I have money left over," she said. "I don't need anything. Everything is paid for. I own my home, I have no debts, so I do fine on $1,200. I just don't know where to put the extra $200."

I advised her to continue putting it in a savings account at her local credit union so she could keep spoiling her grandchildren.

Her story stuck with me because she had such a wonderful life. She loved to spend time in her beautiful garden. She loved to volunteer her time with local charitable organizations. She loved to spend time with her children and grandchildren.

She was one of the most grateful people I've ever met. She was wealthy because she appreciated all the things she had in her life. She was rich by her expectations because she had enough income to take care of all her needs and she didn't have any additional wants.

Being wealthy is not about how much we have, it's

what we believe about what we have. A millionaire can be unhappy and desperate for more, while someone living on $1,400 a month can be totally satisfied with money to spare. The difference between prosperity and poverty is our degree of gratitude.

CHAPTER 2

What Is Your Financial Vision?

People will work hard for money,
but they will die for a cause.

— Mike Teng—

IT HAS BEEN SAID, "Where there is no vision, the people perish." A person will never be financially free unless they have a clear vision of their financial objectives. When you get caught up in the busy expectations of life, it can be hard to take time to reflect and choose your direction, but one of the biggest mistakes people make is trying to navigate their finances without creating a vision first. Your first step to financial freedom begins with a clear Financial Vision Statement.

Definition:
A **Financial Vision Statement** is a positive, passionate description of your financial hopes, bringing them into the present.

Beliefs and habits toward money are part of a family heritage. It's common to treat money the way our parents did. One friend, whose parents declared bankruptcy while he was in college, watched several siblings follow the same course of overspending and financial collapse. Another client still feels guilty buying herself clothes because her mom would often whisper, "Don't tell your dad we went shopping," after each shopping trip.

Other attitudes about money come from the culture. Some people have learned to be passive about their finances. They live paycheck to paycheck, accepting whatever their financial situation is as destiny, as something beyond their control.

Those are my principles. And if you don't like them, I have more.

— Groucho Marx —

Popular financial trends were developed during the Industrial Revolution when many Americans were able to achieve a higher standard of living. This brought new technology, automobiles, airplanes, phones, and television. At first the innovations filled needs, but at some point, the innovations began to provide luxuries. For many people, the luxuries themselves create more stress than enjoyment.

The Origin of Your Beliefs

Does your use of money reflect beliefs created by the media, culture, or your own past?

- Have you ever found yourself thinking that riches equal fulfillment?
- Have you ever found yourself thinking that money equals power?
- Do you find yourself believing that spending equals freedom?
- Do you feel that rich people act selfishly and dishonestly?
- Do you ever feel guilty for having more money than others?
- Do you feel embarrassed when you have less money than your friends?
- When you do have money, does it seem to disappear?

If you answered "yes" to any of the above questions, the media or your past experiences with money may be keeping you from embracing a new vision of your financial future. To get around these mental roadblocks, present your mind with a descriptive vision that impacts you emotionally; a vision that you're passionate about.

More than a decade ago, I met with David from Texas. When it came time to work on his Financial Vision Statement, he was struggling to understand how powerful this statement could be in his life. As I helped him narrow down and adjust the wording, I told David to look at his Financial Vision Statement as if it were a personal contract in his life. David embraced this idea because it really clarified for him how powerful this statement could be. Because of it, everything else in his plan started to make sense.

David's Financial Vision Statement: *"I serve others and enjoy a great life. I surround myself with loving relationships and travel to where I want, with whom I want, and when I want."*

Beth, a single woman in Los Angeles, has faithfully tracked her income and expenses since I began working with her. Her investment portfolio and work benefits have allowed her to enjoy the good life because her money has a purpose. When she came to me twelve years ago, she was in upper management at a Fortune

100 company. Even though she made excellent money, she wasn't satisfied with where she was heading financially—and in her personal relationships.

We started where Beth was in that moment of her life: identifying her strengths and weaknesses and creating a vision for *why* she was doing what she was doing with her life. Since then, she's been able to align her vision with the role her finances play. She is clearly fulfilled in her life because her finances are no longer a concern, and her vision is consistent with what's important to her.

Beth's Financial Vision Statement: *"I spend my time and money with the people I love, building lasting family relationships and experiences. I devote my time, talents, and contributions to the charities of my choice. I live financially free."*

Your Turn:

What is your Financial Vision Statement? To get started, you need to keep five important elements in mind:

1. **Be positive.** When someone tells you not to think of something, how hard is it to get that very thing out of your mind? As you're crafting your statement, focus on what you *do* want, not on what you *don't* want.
2. **Keep it first person.** This is your vision statement. Take ownership of it.
3. **Write in present tense.** The objective is to create conflict between what your senses perceive and your mind envisions. This will tell your subconscious mind that your vision is actually your reality now.
4. **Be emotional.** You need to feel and believe that you've already accomplished your objective. Is your vision statement emotionally moving to you? What effect does reading it have on you? Your heart will not engage in something it can not feel.
5. **Be visionary.** Think long term and look to the top of the mountain. A good vision statement should imprint your desired outcome firmly in your mind and redirect today's wants toward tomorrow's vision.

Most people require a few attempts before they come up with a vision statement that resonates with them. Don't worry if it doesn't come together on your first try—keep working at it. The moment you put the statement of your desire in writing, you take the first in a series of steps that will mentally create the thought into its physical reality.

My wife and I wrote our Financial Vision Statement together: "*We enjoy the abundant life with our money. We are financially secure, independent, and free. We contribute to the lives of others, giving them encouragement, hope, and greater faith in the Lord.*"

Every physical creation begins with a mental creation. These creations are our plans, visualizations, and motives. The truth is that our dreams existed in reality and scientific feasibility all along. Benjamin Franklin did not invent electricity—it was always there. He discovered it. The Wright Brothers didn't invent human flight. They discovered how it could be done. Our dreams already exist. They are waiting for us to bring them into our world.

The secret of success is consistency of purpose.

— Benjamin Disraeli —

More Samples of Financial Vision Statements

"The vision of our money is to provide financial security for our family. We have a beautiful garden with a place to walk, sit, and reflect on the beauty of life. We live within our means, being financially secure. We are full of integrity, commitment, and zeal to live the life we have."

"We love the peace of mind from being financially free. We travel where, when, and how we desire, enjoying the beauties of our world. We enjoy a wonderful life, sharing our abundance with our family, friends, and charities of our choice."

"We rejoice in the financial security we have for ourselves and our family. Our passive income sources sustain our financial security, independence, and freedom. We love assisting others, and helping them learn to improve their financial knowledge."

"Our financial vision is building a legacy of faith, hope, and freedom; and strengthening families. We build leaders and teams with a vision to dream and the courage to be victorious."

"We love life! We love spending time with our children and with each other. We are living a fantastic lifestyle, being able to travel with our family. We are active in our community, serving many others around us."

"We live a secure and full life. We help others achieve the same fulfilling life. We are financially prepared and instill those same values in our children."

"We love the peace of mind our finances give us. We have a wonderful life, surrounded by family, friends, and people we love."

"The purpose of our money is to enjoy a comfortable life. We live in the home of our dreams and enjoy everything about it. Our investments allow us to live at the level we enjoy. With our money, we are generous to the organizations of our choice."

CHAPTER 3

It Is What It Is

Stress comes from knowing what is right
and doing what is wrong.

— Larry Winget —

THE FIRST STEP in making financial progress—or progress in any area of your life—is to do an honest assessment of your current situation. Part of that includes letting go of the past. It doesn't matter what happened before or if there is someone you want to blame for your current situation. All that matters is where you are *right now* and where you want to end up.

During my time in the United States Air Force, I served as a missile launch officer. In the late 1970's, during the Cold War, I was stationed in South Dakota where I worked as a crew member on an ICBM Minuteman missile system.

The integrity of this missile system was contingent upon the missiles being in a state of "strategic alert." In order for the missile to have strategic alert status, the missile, or "sortie," had to know its exact location on the planet at all times. If it didn't know the precise latitude and longitude of its location, it wouldn't be able to reach the pre-programmed target.

As a two-man crew, we monitored fifty missiles in the field at one time. Every eight seconds, each missile was queried electronically, and it would reply electronically to the Launch Control Capsule as to its "strategic alert" status. If, for whatever reason, it did not know its exact coordinates—or sensed another subsystem malfunction, it would immediately go off alert, and we would start the disarming process so the missile could not be launched and the warhead detonated. The reason for these protocols is clear: no nuclear missile would be launched unless it knew exactly where it was going.

Money and missiles have this in common: you can't get where you want to go with your money unless you first know where you are now. And if you don't have a clear idea of where you are, you've essentially disarmed your ability to move forward.

If you're reading this book, you know your financial situation could be improved. Before we can come up with a solution or strategy though, we need to understand and define the situation. For example, a doctor can't prescribe medicine to a patient unless he knows why that patient is ill. The diagnosis precedes the prescription.

That's why honestly assessing your situation—and realizing that "it is what it is"—is such an important first step. You may know that your finances are not in order, but fear is keeping you from sitting down and taking an honest look at your numbers.

When fear is employed, facts are pushed aside. And fear and facts cannot coexist. Once you recognize the truth of your situation, you can then begin to minimize any worries you might have. You face your fear.

If you think education is expensive, try ignorance.

— Benjamin Franklin —

I started working with Gabe and Julie more than a decade ago. When they first came to me, they had a sizable negative net worth. But they were a young family in their early 30's with a lot of motivation and desire to become financially stable.

They were at the point where it was either turn things around or declare bankruptcy.

The first thing we did was deal with their reality. We found out exactly where they were financially strong and where they were financially weak. In their case, they had a good income but far too much debt. Once we figured out those and other details, we looked at how Gabe and Julie managed their cash flow; what was working and what wasn't.

Then we created a Financial Vision Statement (see Chapter 2 to write your own). From there, I helped them develop a realistic plan that they could agree upon and get excited about.

In two years, they'd progressed from a substantial negative net worth to over $10,000 in net worth. In the following few years, life threw some curve balls at Gabe and Julie. However, they did a great job being resilient because they knew exactly where they were—and where they wanted to end up.

Face Your Fears:

1. What is a financial problem or concern you have at this moment? ______________________

2. What are three possible solutions to that concern?

____

____

____

3. In your opinion, which of those three solutions is the best or most plausible choice? ______________

____

Sample answers:

1. What is a financial problem or concern you have at this moment? *I don't have enough savings to take care of my family if something happens to my earning capability.*

2. What are three possible solutions to that concern?
    - *Get a second job for extra income now.*
    - *Add to my savings reserve account.*
    - *Pay off high interest/low balance debt.*

3. In your opinion, which of those three solutions is the best or most plausible one? *Add to the savings reserve—because that's one I can do immediately to alleviate the worry as I work toward my long-term goals.*

Jake and Molly came to me when they were in their 40's. The first thing we did was establish where they were financially.

They had a few decades of marriage behind them, which meant they'd had plenty of time to make financial progress, as well as make some financial mistakes. They overspent at times, didn't create a reserve fund, and were not paying attention to their 401k plans.

Once their current situation was established, we looked at their strengths and weaknesses. Then we formulated a plan that would be consistent with their Financial Vision Statement.

Like Gabe and Julie, Jake and Molly had to fend off a few financial curve balls. Throughout those ups and downs, they stuck to their plan and stayed focused on their vision. Now they're well on the road to retiring in their late 50's and able to give appropriate assistance to their adult children, something that has always been important to them.

Jake and Molly will never be millionaires—because they don't want to be. They just want a good family life with sufficient income to support their lifestyle. Since they embraced their current reality, they're able to control their financial future.

The Difference Between Achievement & Success

People often tie success to achievement but I believe there is an important distinction between those two terms. *Achievement* refers to something you've accomplished. For example, that could include major life milestones, awards, bonuses, or accomplishing life goals.

Success, on the other hand, is a feeling of accomplishment. If I ask, "Are you successful?" I don't need to know your achievements, your job description, or your family details, because ultimately, your level of success depends on how you feel about your life.

Gabe and Julie could consider themselves very successful because they tackled their debt and took control of their finances. It doesn't matter that their net worth was only $10,000 at that given time.

If you *feel* you're successful, then you *are* successful.

What Your Money Says About You

Money is neither good nor evil. It's simply a medium used to exchange goods and services.

One reason people resist financial coaching is because it is a reflection of what they really value, and it can be excruciatingly painful to one's self-image.

You probably know someone who lives in a big house and drives a nice car but is overwhelmed with personal debt. You may know someone who spends their paycheck on frivolous things as soon as they are paid, or someone who constantly complains about how broke they are, even while amassing large sums of money.

It's not their money's fault those people are struggling; it's their belief about their money. When it comes to our finances, there are no victims or martyrs. People do the best they know how to do. We're all willing participants in our economic lives.

The question is: when life throws those curve balls at you, do you stand there and let them knock you down? Or do you do whatever it takes to figure things out and move forward once again?

Many people react to hardships by beating themselves up. They spend time disapproving of the mistakes they made, obsessing over what they did wrong and punishing themselves for falling short of perfection. How much time do you spend beating yourself up over your financial mistakes?

When you spend time beating yourself up, progress is reversed. You don't just stop moving forward—you actually move backward.

In Chapter 4, *Recognizing Reality*, you will be introduced to a Financial Independence Profile, which will help you assess your current financial situation. Once you understand that your situation is what it is, you'll not only jump start your way to becoming financially free, you may find yourself actually enjoying the process as well.

CHAPTER 4

Recognizing Reality

If you cannot see reality, you cannot embrace opportunity.

— John W. Schott —

As part of my graduate studies in counseling, I worked with drug and alcohol addicts. One thing you learn quickly is that progress is simply not possible if the patient is unwilling to recognize the reality of their situation. When they recognized the reality—that they had a drug or alcohol problem—then progress could be made.

Recognizing reality is one of the most difficult and challenging things people will tackle in their lives. All of us have a natural resistance to change, creating patterns of avoidance and withdrawal from painful areas. When it comes to personal finance, our society compounds the problem by not educating the next generation on how to manage money, let alone recognize the reality of their specific situation. Our high schools don't teach these skills. Our colleges don't teach these skills. Credit card companies certainly don't teach them either.

Fewer than ten percent of American adults understand how their 401k works thoroughly enough to explain it to someone else. Most Americans have no idea what a net worth is, let alone what *their* net worth is.

TOTAL ASSETS minus TOTAL LIABILITIES = NET WORTH

The dollar figure that sums up your financial net worth is an important indicator of your monetary health. This is calculated by adding up everything you own and subtracting everything you owe; your assets minus your liabilities. This number, your "net worth," determines in large measure your ability to accomplish your financial goals. It affects your retirement plans, the home you live in, the trips you take, and the cars you buy.

Let's be honest. Figuring out this number is a little like getting on the bathroom scale after the holidays. You may discover you're heavily in debt and until this moment, you would have escaped facing the hard truth. On the other hand, you may discover that you're closer to financial security than you would have imagined. There's no correct or incorrect answer here. You don't have to compare your number with the "Joneses" next door. But holding yourself to a standard of thoroughness, honesty, and accuracy at this step is the only way to ensure you're traveling down the right path.

Remember:

Your financial net worth has absolutely no correlation to your personal worth as an individual.

When Jim came to visit me shortly after the market downturn in 2000, he was badly in need of financial advice. He'd been laid off, as many computer programmers were, and to keep his family afloat, he'd been living off his savings, along with a home equity line of credit and credit cards. Now that he was working again, he'd gathered up the courage to assess his situation.

The first thing we looked at was his house. He owed $235,000 on a home that could barely sell for that amount. In fact, after listing it with a Realtor, he would net much less than what he needed to break even. He had eaten up all of the equity by using a home equity line of credit to support his family while he was unemployed. But he loved his house. He bought the home he grew up in, and it was worth more than money to him. So he decided to keep it.

Second, we totaled the amount owed on his credit cards. He was astonished to learn he'd racked up nearly $50,000. For several years, he had juggled balances between the cards, maintaining high balances on low interest introductory rate cards. But that game was getting harder to play, and late payments ruined his credit score. A new law allowing credit card companies to raise rates—even if you're late on an unrelated loan—sent all of his rates skyrocketing.

The good news about his cars: he owned them outright. When he added it all up, or rather subtracted it, his net worth came to -$50,000. His situation was grim, but it was an immense relief to him just knowing where he stood. Knowing allowed him to make a plan to change his situation.

You can recover from financially difficult times. After an economic downturn and failed business venture, Abraham Lincoln worked for many years to repay his debts. The character he developed in those years served our country well.

Not all my clients had to overcome such bleak circumstances. Mike and Kathy were also surprised by the results of their Financial Independence Plan, but in a positive way. They stopped tracking their investment statements a few years before they met with me. It was just too disheartening for them to see how much they'd lost during the market slump—and to see how slowly it was coming back. They'd always planned to retire at 60, but they weren't sure if that was possible anymore.

In January of 2005, when they sat down to do their profile, they discovered that their IRAs had regained almost all of the former values. They were thrilled to see their investments were back up to $322,000, but they still had work to do. There were credit cards to pay down and a home equity line of credit to pay off. (Take a look at Mike and Kathy's Financial Independence Profile on the next page.)

FINANCIAL INDEPENDENCE PROFILE

Peace of Mind Savings: $22,000
Objective

Mike & Kathy Sample • November 5, 2014
3824 Orchard Drive, Sandy, UT 84093
801-278-3645 • mksample@gmail.com

Cash Assets

Institution	Purpose	Type	%	Ownership	Value
Chase Bank	Business	Checking	0.00%	Kathy	2,000
Delta Credit Union	Household	Checking	1.00%	JT	1,500
Bank of America	Reserves	Savings	1.50%	JT	18,000
Wells Fargo	Tax Reserves	Business	0.00%	JT	3,000
				TOTAL	**$24,500**

Invested Assets

Company	Purpose	Product	%	Ownership	Value
Pershing	College Fund	Stock	5.00%	JT	19,000
Pershing	Cabin	EFT's	6.00%	JT	55,000
Delta—Fidelity	Retirement	EFT's	4.00%	401K-M	308,500
Sample Ent.—TD Am	Retirement	EFT's	7.00%	401K-K	62,000
Pershing	Retirement	EFT's	6.00%	IRA-K	35,000
Ameritas Life Insurance	Family Bank	Cash Value - Life...	5.00%	Mike	19,240
Silver Rounds	Investment	Precious Metals	8.50%	JT	22,500
				TOTAL	**$521,240**

Use Assets

Item	Description	Value
Home	3824 Orchard Drive	320,000
Furnishings		50,000
Vehicle	2013 Toyota Camry	19,000
Vehicle	2012 Jeep Cherokee	16,000
Sailboat	Hobie Cat	8,000
Recreational Property	Quail Lake	10,000
Other		
Other		
	TOTAL	**$423,000**

Liabilities

Institution	Year &Term	Type	%	Paymnt	Balance
Bank of America	2006—15 yrs	1st Mortgage	3.50	1,250	195,000
Key Bank	2009—open	Home Equity LOC	4.00	350	12,000
Visa		Credit Card	10.00	200	6,500
Mastercard		Credit Card	12.50	150	4,000
TOTALS				**$1,950**	**$217,500**
Net Worth					**$751,240**

Board of Advisors

Financial Advisor/Coach	Greg Kesten, 801-565-0262
Attorney	Mary Steinberg
Accountant	Chris Anderson
Property & Casualty Agent	Roberta Stenson
Trust & Wills Dated	7/1/14
Risk—Reward Tolerance	Conservative

Family Profile

Name	DOB	Status	Age
Mike	06/03/51		63
Kathy	02/09/52		62
Chris	11/16/79	son, married + 2	34
Patrice	10/21/82	daughter, single	32
Marcus	03/14/87	son, single, at home	27

Income

Name	Company	Annual (est)
Mike	Delta	$72,000
Kathy	Sample Enterprises	$54,000
	TOTAL	**$126,000**

Tax

	2013	2014(est)
Form 1040 line 22—Total Income	118,468	121,000
Form 1040 line 43—Taxable Income	82,355	87,000

Financial Objectives

Target Date mm/yy	Amount required	Description
September 1, 2019	$217,500	Debt free for life
May 1, 2020	$75,000	Cabin at Quail Lake
January 1, 2021	$1,000,000	Cash & Invested Assets

When we argue with reality,
we lose 100 percent of the time.

– Janet Atwood –

Your first responsibility with your money is to live within your means. Your total inflow should be more than your total outflow over a period of time. Being "wealthy" is about appreciating your quality of life, while being "rich" is simply a function of your financial net worth.

Most people are already wealthy because our modern society provides so many with so much. People who recognize the true source of wealth have a greater sense of well-being in their life. Once you understand that, the question becomes: how *rich* do you want to be and what price are you willing to pay for your freedom?

CHAPTER 5

The Comparison Killer

Comparison is the death of joy.

— Mark Twain —

It's the latest gadget and you don't have it—but your neighbor does. You try to find out more. When did he get it? Where did he buy it? How much did it cost? Your questions are friendly but inside your stomach is churning with envy. You feel inadequate, self-conscious, like you're missing out—and these feelings are killing you.

These are the feelings we bring up when we compare ourselves to others. We all do it in different ways. Perhaps you want to drive the best car in your neighborhood, and when your friend pulls up in a Mustang Cobra, you start calculating how to fit an extra car payment into your budget.

Maybe you clean and organize your house like your

very life depends on it and when you visit someone who does it better, you rush home in a panic to duplicate or top what you just saw.

Maybe your image of being a successful breadwinner includes dressing your spouse and children in designer clothes, regardless of the impact this has on your family cash flow.

Maybe the birthday parties you throw for your children are so flawless and perfectly executed, you sleep soundly at night knowing no one else comes close.

Whatever your specific comparison crutch is, it's important to identify it, examine it, and let it go. There will always be someone with more money than you. There will always be someone with far less. You can look down your nose at those who don't measure up and feel confident and secure, maybe even arrogant. But you'll inevitably run into someone who's higher up on the financial food chain.

What then?

Who *should* we compare ourselves to?

Why do we need to compare ourselves to others at all?

How much time he gains who does not look
to see what his neighbor says or does or thinks,
but only at what he does himself.

— Marcus Aurelius —

Most people don't realize how much of their self-worth is tied up in their net-worth. Consequently, they spend most of their lives comparing themselves to everyone around them—not to the people who have less than they have, but those who have more. And thanks to the technological advances in our culture, we have more opportunities than ever to feel inferior. Social media, endless television shows and movies, tabloids and magazines fill our lives with stories and snapshots of the wealthiest, luckiest, most talented, and beautiful people walking the earth.

Your Turn:

Turn on your TV and watch the first three commercials you come across. Write down what they were advertising and how it made you feel.

More than likely, the main message is that you need more. You need more retirement savings. You need shinier hair. You need a faster car.

These are popular advertising tools because they work. They aren't appealing to your logical mind. They are appealing to your emotions, your feelings of inadequacy.

What would your life look like if you didn't compare yourself to others? What would your life look like if you accepted your circumstances with gratitude and understanding?

Comparison robs you of your freedom to enjoy all that you have because your entire focus is on what you *don't* have. In the words of Iyanla Vanzant, "Comparison is an act of violence against the self." It causes you to beat yourself—and others—down.

Years ago, I worked with Linda, a middle-aged woman in the Chicago area, who was married with three children. Her main financial struggles came from her tendency to compare herself to others. It bled into all areas of her life: her finances, her home, her clothes, even the accomplishments of her children.

Linda and her husband earned a substantial income, but she constantly overspent in an effort to keep up with those around her. The biggest trap she fell into was comparing herself to people who had more than she did. Her home was beautiful, but it wasn't the largest one in her circle of friends, so she needed to upgrade.

When she heard about her sister's amazing vacation, she set about planning an even better one. This habit of comparing and spending put a major strain on their finances, but she was unwilling to make even modest compromises to secure a healthy financial future.

For example, in one of our sessions, she revealed that she was too broke to buy a birthday present for her niece.

"How many nieces do you have?" I asked her.

"About ten nieces and ten nephews between all my siblings," she said.

"What is the typical expectation for a birthday present?"

"I spend $50 per niece and nephew on their birthday."

"That's $1,000 a year just in birthday presents," I told her. "It's no wonder, with that kind of expectation, that you feel so much pressure."

I advised her to tell her family she would no longer participate in the birthday gift exchange. She refused to consider the idea because she knew her family would think something was wrong with her. There *was* something wrong. She was so focused on comparing herself to others and keeping up the appearance of wealth that she was spending herself into bankruptcy. She could live the fantasy, but if she didn't face the issue, her need to compare would eventually kill her financial future.

Another time, I worked with Scott, a man who lived in Georgia. His father, whom Scott respected and loved more than anyone in his life, was a harsh disciplinarian. He expected Scott to excel in school, sports, and as a member of the community.

Scott grew up always feeling that he needed to be the best, most respected person in his circle. Whenever he was lacking, he used his money to make up the difference. Though he was a good man, working hard in his professional life and donating time and money to local community groups and charitable organizations, he couldn't stop comparing himself to others. For Scott, having what he had was not as important to him as making sure he had more than other people. Instead of enjoying the fruits of his hard work and the love of the community he does so much for, he lived in a constant state of stress, with no hope of financial fulfillment.

Ask yourself: how much is enough? If your objective is to simply spend *more* than the people around you, you'll never achieve financial freedom. Instead of looking out toward everyone else, consider looking inward.

Your value as a person does not have a dollar sign in front of it. You will never be better than everyone else. You will never be worse than everyone else. It's time to stop measuring, comparing, and killing yourself to keep up.

How much do you compare yourself to others? Here are some questions to consider:

- Do you ever feel anxious or inadequate when you compare your financial situation with someone else's?
- Does it make you feel insecure if someone around you achieves any measure of success?
- Do you experience a feeling of envy when you see someone buy something that's better than what you have?
- Do you spend time fantasizing or dreaming about things you will not have, like lavish vacations or luxurious cars?
- Do you ever feel that if you buy certain things, you'll be more liked or accepted?

If you answered "yes" to any of these questions, you may be caught in the comparison killer trap. Next time you find yourself doing it, stop, recognize what you're doing, and turn your thoughts to the things you're grateful for. If you don't, constantly comparing yourself to others could kill your chance at a secure financial future.

Whether you're as poor as a has-been reality star or as rich as Bill Gates, you can be financially free. Our feelings of being "less than" are caused by comparison to others. The only comparison you should make is your former self to your current self.

CHAPTER 6

Cash Flow is King

There is no dignity quite so impressive,
and no one independence quite so important,
as living within your means.

— Calvin Coolidge —

You probably know, and can easily recall, how much money you made last month. But do you know how much you spent? Many Americans spend ten percent more than they make, in part because they have such a difficult time tracking their spending.

We live in a nearly cashless society. Using a debit or credit card is fast and effortless, but it's also easy to lose track of your spending that way. Keeping accurate records of your outflow can be difficult and a hassle. But keeping these records will increase your motivation to accomplish your financial goals. A few minutes a day tracking your money will "pay" you far more than the time you spent working to earn it. The average savings generated from cash flow management exercises can be anywhere from a couple hundred dollars to several thousand per month.

Most of us would agree that it's vital for corporations to have a current profit/loss statement. Without this, the company would easily overspend and accrue heavy debt loads. With no plan in place, it's unlikely that cash reserves would be available when necessary. A company functioning in the red won't stay in business for very long.

Families can often slip into overspending without realizing it. Credit and borrowing opportunities are abundant and overspending can go on for months before the credit card bills become a burden. Then out of the blue, those credit card limits are exceeded and there's not enough cash to pay the bills.

Poor is a condition that is very sad.
Broke is because you're under-earning or over-spending.
We can fix broke.

— Larry Winget —

Increase Your Cash Flow

If you're stuck in a financial rut, one option would be to increase your cash flow, but many people find it hard to come up with viable ways to do this. Actually, there are limitless options for increasing your cash flow. Only your ability and motivation is required for the possibilities to manifest themselves.

Although you may increase your headaches as you increase your income (after all, money doesn't solve problems, people do), it can add some discretionary funds to part of your monthly cash flow.

Some ways to generate extra income include:

- Having investments in high interest-bearing or dividend-producing assets.
- Working more hours at your current employment.
- Take a passion or hobby and develop it into a business model that will produce income.
- Add a second source of income to your primary employment.

Financially free people are doers, not complainers. Those who struggle with finances are complainers, not doers. So if you need or want to generate more cash flow, go out and do it.

Decrease Your Spending

One way to decrease spending—you can always quit eating. Unfortunately this method tends to make you weak and dizzy, so it's probably not a practical solution. For those of us who need food to survive, there are some other strategies to save money. If you're willing to make appropriate adjustments and change your habits, you'll quickly change your financial state. For those who only make small changes, it typically takes more time to see results.

Exercise: Where are the Financial Leaks in Your Cash Flow?

- Shop your phone bill and eliminate non-essential features.
- Review your current auto, home, health, and life insurance policies to make sure you have the best premium or rate and coverage for your needs. Combine insurance with the same company for a possible discount.
- Eliminate or reduce your cable TV service. Use the library for books, DVDs, and music.
- Find a bank or credit union with free checking, online banking, and automatic bill pay. Get a no fee credit line instead of overdraft protection. Never use an ATM that charges you a fee.
- Always shop with a grocery list. Use coupons. Cook more. Freeze leftovers. Brown bag your lunch. Cut out your morning coffee run.
- Downsize your residence.
- Buy good quality used cars instead of new. Carpool or use public transit.

- Turn down the heat and wear a sweater; turn off the air conditioner and use a fan.
- Exercise for free: walk, bike, jog, or get a workout video.
- Never finance furniture!
- Turn your hot water heater down and wrap it with insulation.
- Shop around for the best prescription rates, including mail order companies.
- Negotiate your credit card rates and stop carrying your credit cards around with you.
- Remember, if you don't see it, you won't buy it.

Mary, an admitted spendaholic, reluctantly agreed to track all of her expenses. When she began writing them down, she received a big surprise.

"It was a disaster," she said. "I realized I had no idea where my money was going. Even after writing everything down for a month, I couldn't make the numbers add up. There was still $800 unaccounted for."

Mary is not alone. There are many people who experience the same cash flow issues. During the first few months keeping track of your expenses, you may find that the figures don't seem to add up. As you continue to write down where you spend your money, you'll notice the amount of slippage decreases, and the accuracy of your cash flow management increases.

Tracking your spending is the key to reducing any spending leaks.

In the first month of tracking their inflow and outflow, Lisa and Curtis discovered their outflow total was greater than their inflow. They knew they'd had a few bad habits but it was disappointing to see the reality laid out on paper. They were having trouble keeping up with their bills, and their credit card balances had been increasing every month. So they committed themselves to doing better.

They cut back on shopping trips and eating at expensive restaurants. They reduced the number of costly dates, including season tickets to the theater and season passes to amusement parks. They paid attention to their expenses with the determination of improving their situation. They succeeded! When they entered their expense figure the next month, they noticed a substantial reduction in spending.

But they couldn't sustain their new habits and in the third month, their expenses rebounded with a vengeance. Discouraged, they were ready to give up.

They wanted to change their habits but didn't want to give up the quality of life they'd become accustomed to.

Lisa and Curtis decided to begin again, this time taking a more realistic approach. They examined their motives for purchases, giving up what was less important to them while retaining things that brought them fulfillment. They learned to take unexpected expenses in stride and pay cash for them instead of avoiding them through credit.

Too many people spend money they haven't earned, to buy things they don't want, to impress people they don't like.

— Will Smith —

For Mike and Kathy, the excitement of the cash flow analysis came when they discovered how much of their money was disappearing to what they called, "stupid stuff." Every weekend Kathy rented three or four movies for their children, but they would often end up not watching them. They were tossing away $9 a month for their checking account fees and $5 a month to pay for online banking. Kathy's cappuccino each morning cost her $6.

As they started keeping track of their purchases, they became more aware of where their money was going. This helped them slow the leaks.

CASH FLOW MANAGEMENT WORKSHEET SAMPLE
(Mike & Kathy • November 5, 2014)

		Jul-14	Aug-14	Sep-14	Oct-14	Nov-14	Dec-14
INFLOW							
Name	**Company**	**actual**	**actual**	**actual**	**actual**	**est.**	**est.**
Mike	Delta	$5,800	$5,800	$5,800	$5,800	$5,800	
Kathy	Sample Enterprises	$4,600	$4,600	$4,600	$4,600	$4,600	
	Total Inflow	$10,400	$10,400	$10,400	$10,400	$10,400	$ -
OUTFLOW							
Withholdings and/or business expenses	FICA-Social Security	$800	$800	$900	$900	$850	
	FITW – Fed Tax	$1,100	$1,100	$1,125	$1,125	$1,100	
	State Tax	$200	$200	$220	$220	$210	
	Medicare	$50	$50	$65	$65	$60	
	Delta 401(k)	$800	$800	$800	$800	$800	
	Business-misc.	$100	$100	$100	$100	$100	
	Sub Total	$3,050	$3,050	$3,210	$3,210	$3,120	$ -
	NET INCOME	**$7,350**	**$7,350**	**$7,190**	**$7,190**	**$7,280**	**$ -**
Fixed	Home Mortgage (PITI)	$1,250	$1,250	$1,250	$1,250	$1,250	
	Auto Loan	$350	$350	$350	$350	$350	
	Sub Total	$1,600	$1,600	$1,600	$1,600	$1,600	$ -
Variable	Contributions	$700	$900	$700	$600	$700	
	Savings	$800	$800	$800	$800	$800	
	Groceries	$425	$400	$410	$385	$400	
	Utilities	$300	$325	$275	$250	$300	
	Auto: gas, oil, etc.	$220	$230	$210	$220	$210	
	Phone,internet,cable	$180	$160	$170	$155	$170	
	Personal Care	$375	$395	$335	$340	$350	
	Clothing	$300			$375		
	Insurance:auto,home,health,life	$850	$1,050	$700	$800	$800	
	Sub Total	$4,150	$4,260	$3,600	$3,925	$3,730	$ -
Discretionary	Travel/Vacation	$1,150	$500	$320	$300	$1,030	
	Gifts	$50	$100	$500	$445	$400	
	Entertainment	$150	$150	$300	$300	$30	
	Dining Out	$200	$200	$200	$200	$200	
	Sub Total	$1,550	$950	$1,320	$1,245	$1,660	$ -
	TOTAL EXPENSES	$7,300	$6,810	$6,520	$6,770	$6,990	$ -
	Difference (+ or -)	$50	$540	$670	$420	$290	$ -
	Reconciling sources:						
	Credit card charge						
	Reconciled Difference (+)	$50	$540	$670	$420	$290	$ -

Many Americans struggle with getting financially ahead. Every time our income increases, our expenses increase accordingly. We buy more expensive cars, plan bigger vacations, and upgrade our houses. In college, my necessities were tuition, books, a place to sleep at night, and a big box of Cheerios. Today, my list of "necessary expenses" seems endless.

How much of our necessities are really necessary? Seventy percent of the world's population lives on $2 or less a day. I have one good friend whose "necessary" expenses haven't changed since college. Her husband left his high-paying programming job when he was activated by the National Guard, and even on military pay, her family was able to save $4,000 a year.

Living a simple life isn't for everyone, but their's is an inspiring example. Shrinking our definition of what's essential to our quality of life affords us more freedom to accomplish our objectives.

Work on your own cash flow and be completely honest with yourself. As you're looking at your cash flow, question every expense. Look at your necessities as well as your discretionary expenses and make a list of areas where you can conserve money. Try to find at least six areas in which to make an adjustment.

Imagine you are only able to free-up $10 a day. The only thing you were willing to give up was your morning coffee and bagel before work. That's $50 a week, $2,600 a year and, over ten years, it adds up to more than $30,000 if you earn five percent interest per year in a dividend producing investment.

Now that makes sense! Who said managing your cash flow was boring?

Wealthy people seek to maintain their well-being by saying "yes" to things that support their objectives and "no" to things that take them off track.

Financial security is living within your means. Living *above* your means leads to stress, or worse. One is the recipe for contentment. The other is a recipe for frustration. You'll find the freedom to accomplish your financial objectives if you can develop the discipline to direct your cash toward the things that matter most.

CHAPTER 7

The Spending Addiction

A bargain is something you can't use at a price you can't resist.

— Franklin Jones —

ARE YOU TRAINED TO BE A CUSTOMER, always spending your money?

We've all noticed how stores jump from one holiday event to the next. As soon as the Fourth of July is over, the Back to School signs are put up. After Labor Day, Halloween decorations are out and well before Thanksgiving arrives, Christmas is on display.

This is a necessary approach for businesses hoping to draw in customers, but how much have we, as a society, internalized their consumer-driven timeline? Are you always thinking of the next holiday or event you need to buy presents for? Do you overspend for special occasions, feel guilty, vow to do better, but as soon as you save a bit of money, you are back to spending it all again?

This is known as the spending addiction.

It's something most consumers go through. We spend so we can have something. Then we save—so we can spend money to buy something else. It's a cycle that's very difficult to break.

We become addicted to spending—addicted to buying holiday presents, birthday gifts, vacation packages, anniversary celebrations. We plan for our necessary and ordinary expenses (groceries, utilities, miscellaneous payments), but we're constantly faced with the need to buy things above and beyond that.

We don't realize that more is never enough. Just as stores begin to advertise the next holiday the moment one is over, we turn our attention to the next thing we don't have as soon as the rush of buying something new fades.

Ultimately, all we need for a given lifestyle is to have sufficient for our needs. Everything above that is optional or unnecessary. When we're caught in the spending addiction, we accumulate things quicker than we consume them. Do you know someone who parks their cars on the street or in their driveway because their garage is full of stuff? People have whole closets, whole rooms, or whole basements filled with things they're not using, even as they go out and buy more.

When I was in Samoa for two years, I lived out of a 2 x 2 x 3 wooden box. Fales (or Samoan homes) didn't typically have walls, just a floor and a roof held up by poles. There was efficiency to the way people lived there. You couldn't keep track of much stuff so you learned not to accumulate it. As I moved from village to village, living with different families, all I had, all I needed was in my 2 x 2 x 3 wooden box. It was easy to pick up and go.

It made me realize that when we need to, or when we *want* to, we can live on very little. When you're trapped in a spending addiction, you can never become financially free because you are addicted to what you want, not what you have.

One client I worked with was a salesperson for a large company. Jared did very well financially. But he was always thinking about ways to spend his money in the here and now, rather than saving for any long-term objectives.

Consequently, Jared always spent his money to get short-term pleasure. Then he'd feel guilty and try to accelerate paying down his loans and credit card bills. He felt obligated to be a good provider to his family. To him, that meant big holidays, cruises, gifts—even a second home that required him to take on the obligation of another monthly mortgage.

In the course of our sessions, he realized he had a spending addiction. The first step to breaking any addiction is to realize that you have one.

From there, what do you do next?

In Jared's case, he felt so compelled to please and indulge his family, that he was unable to break the cycle. He continued spending, and spending, and spending some more.

Eventually, Jared went bankrupt.

Simply knowing that he shouldn't spend so much on unnecessary extras wasn't enough to inspire Jared to change his ways. He needed a vision of the future to hold to when temptation struck.

The antidote to the spending addiction is simple.

You create a vision of what you really want. This makes you focus on bigger, long-term objectives instead of obsessing about the next special occasion.

If there's a big enough WHY, the "what" and "how" will happen.

If you want to take your family on a special vacation, and you know you need to save a certain amount to do that, it becomes easier to say "no" to smaller purchases, or to trim back how much you spend on extras.

Another example could be a family that has a set budget amount for presents to each other. When you predetermine that amount, you're less likely to overspend. For instance, if you decide to only spend $300 on gifts for each family member during the holidays, you know to set the money aside. Then when the holiday arrives, that money is already there, ready for you to enjoy. This breaks the cycle of spending, saving to pay off credit cards, then racking up more credit card debt when the next holiday comes around.

If you have an overall objective or specific goal, you're less apt to spend imprudently. A dollar spent on impulse is a dollar taken from your financial vision.

Clark, a policeman from Ohio, was very frugal with his money. His wife, Jane, on the other hand, was a spendthrift. When I began working with them, I realized right away that she had a spending addiction. So I emphasized the importance of having a viable cash flow management plan.

Clark put together a sophisticated plan that accounted for every dollar that came in, and tracked where every dollar was spent. He was excited about this plan and kept at it, month after month. But the family was still consistently spending more than they brought in.

The core issue was that they kept buying things they could postpone for later, but decided to purchase now. Double pane windows. A backyard barbecue. Piano lessons. Gifts for family members. A new car. There was always something to spend the money on.

Clark and Jane would argue about their plan and objectives. He wanted to save and pay down debt. She agreed with that idea in theory, but worried if they didn't buy what she wanted now, they never would. It put enormous pressure on them, and they eventually quit their financial coaching. Their different approaches to money caused too much discouragement and conflict. He was addicted to saving, and she was addicted to spending.

If they had understood that money is not security, they wouldn't have had so much anxiety about whether they were saving enough or buying enough. Instead of fighting about their different approaches, they could have put more time and energy into developing satisfying and lasting relationships with the ones they love.

Do you have a spending addiction?

1. If you bring in extra money, is your first thought a list of things you could spend it on?

2. Do you tend to borrow money, instead of saving money, so you don't have to wait to buy the things you want?

3. Do you get upset if anyone questions how you spend your money?

4. Do you worry about buying gifts for holidays and special occasions months in advance?

5. As soon as one holiday is over, do you immediately start planning what to buy for the next occasion?

6. Do you feel guilty after the satisfaction of spending fades?

If you answered "yes" to three or more of these questions, you might have a spending addiction.

Maya was referred to me when she was a young, single woman. She wanted to do certain things with her life, but she didn't know how to afford them. We worked over the months to set up goals and find feasible ways to obtain them.

She started saving more money, sold some assets, got out of debt and cut back on unnecessary expenses. She was willing to do all the things she needed to do in order to obtain her goal of moving across the country.

As she implemented the monthly cash flow program that we set up together, she found it was easier than she expected to avoid spending money on anything that took away from her objectives.

Much to her surprise, she met her financial goals more quickly than she imagined. Now she is debt free, has a healthy cash flow, is enjoying her brand new car, and lives where she's always wanted to live.

Why did Maya succeed where others failed? Maya had one major advantage over some of my other clients: she was able to keep the WHY in the forefront of her mind. She knew *why* she wanted to save her money so she figured out *what* she needed to do and then *how* to do it.

When the WHY is big enough, the WHAT and HOW will happen. We are emotional beings. Most of our decisions are based on emotions so we tend to accomplish the most when we are emotionally committed to something better.

CHAPTER 8

The Paranoid Saver

The opposite of happiness is not unhappiness. It is worry.

— Anonymous —

JUST AS SOMEONE can be addicted to spending, there are those who go too far in the other direction. Some people are so concerned they don't have enough money, they constantly worry about their savings. They're paralyzed by fear, always preparing for the worst case scenario, always "pulling up the plant to see how the roots are doing," as the saying goes.

Another word to describe this kind of person is a "catastrophizer." They are seldom accurate in their fears, and when they are, on occasion correct, it becomes a self-fulfilling prophecy.

It's difficult to enjoy life when you're constantly worried about what bad thing could happen next. Mark Twain once said, "Worrying is like paying a debt you don't owe."

The antidote to being a paranoid saver is to have a solid financial plan in place where appropriate adjustments can be made and peace of mind is realized.

Which is worse, the addicted spender or the paranoid saver? The answer is: whatever you might be. Spending yourself into bankruptcy will lead to misery. However, it's just as bad to be so focused on saving for the future, you never enjoy the moment.

Saving/Spending Continuum

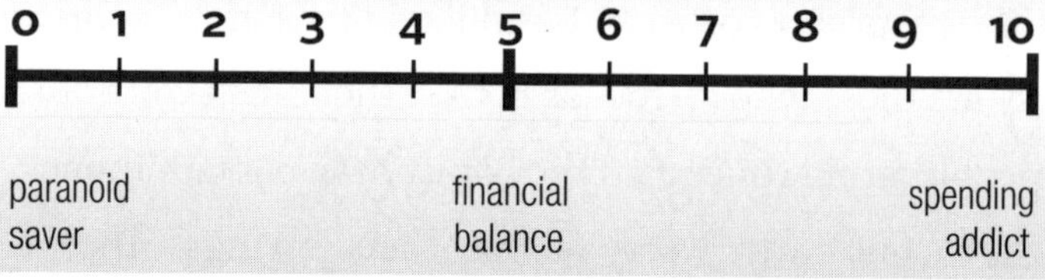

I had one client who liked to meet with me on a regular basis. Matt would drop by my office about once a week just to go over his financial plan and check in on his investments. The last time I saw him was on a Thursday afternoon.

Matt was a perfect example of someone who kept "pulling up the plant to see how the roots were doing." He was a great guy who constantly worried about his finances. He was always concerned he wasn't saving enough for retirement.

I still remember the last Thursday I spent with

Matt. The meeting proceeded as usual, but because of time constraints, we made plans to meet the following Monday. On Sunday, I received a call from Matt's adult daughter. While mowing his lawn the day before, Matt had a massive heart attack and died.

How much of your life are you trading for money? What is the cost of your career ambition and all the things you must have in order to continue in your career progression? What kind of lifestyle would you have if you spent less of your life energy on making and saving money?

If you're so busy making money and worrying about the future that you don't have time to do the things you want to do today, then you're not free.

I started working with Nick about thirty years ago. We became friends quickly. We would talk about money, politics, current events, and anything else we could think of.

Nick would put in more than fifty hours a week at his engineering job. His focus on working and saving money was so singular that he didn't have time for friends, and he alienated most of his family members.

Like Matt, Nick was focused on saving for his retirement. He was a very intelligent man with a good grasp of macroeconomics so he knew exactly what he wanted to accumulate for his retirement.

As I worked with Nick over the years, he became a multimillionaire. He was very rich, but not very wealthy. He was so focused on saving and working that he neglected his relationships, leading to many familial estrangements and two divorces. He also didn't take very good care of himself, and his health got progressively worse.

Nick didn't know how to enjoy his money because he was always planning for a rainy day and worrying about the future. He retired in his early 70's but was only able to enjoy the fruits of his labor for about a year and a half before he passed away from a stroke.

Nick was a good man, however he never could shake the paranoid feeling that he didn't have enough money. His trust and will was not current when he passed away. His third wife passed away a few years later so his children ended up going to court to fight over the millions he left behind.

Nick never enjoyed his money in life. And his children were unable to enjoy it after his death.

Are you a paranoid saver?

1. If you have extra money, is your first thought "where should I save it?"

2. Do you save up money to buy something and then have a hard time actually spending the money once you have it?

3. Do you get upset if anyone questions why and where you save your money?

4. Do you worry about spending money on gifts for holidays and special occasions months in advance?

5. Do you resent having spent money on someone after realizing the favor was not reciprocated to the same degree?

6. Do you feel that what you've saved is never enough?

If you answered "yes" to three or more of these questions, you might be a paranoid saver.

Planning and saving for the future is important. However, you will want to enjoy the moment and find joy in your life through both expected and unexpected events.

As Konrad Adenauer once said, "We all live under the same sky, but we don't all have the same horizon." There is more than one way to measure profit and loss. All the money in the world cannot bring you happiness if you don't know how to let go of fear and worry, living in the here and now.

CHAPTER 9

Horseradish on Your Ice Cream

Over the long term, independent thinking is the surest path to riches and wealth.

— Anonymous —

One of the great freedoms in life is being able to choose who we want to be and what we want to do. We use the term "lifestyle" to describe these different choices. However, a person's lifestyle is more than just choices. It is based on their deeply personal belief system.

There will be many times in our lives when we're faced with a good choice versus another good choice. At that point, it becomes a matter of preference or what particular thing we think makes life worth living.

When someone makes a personal choice that I perhaps wouldn't have made, I like to say, "Some people just want horseradish on their ice cream."

Although I don't see the horseradish on my

ice cream, who am I to point out other people's horseradish? If they like it, why shouldn't they have it? Financially speaking, when a person manages their cash flow properly, they have the opportunity to spend their money on what appeals to them. What appeals to them will be different than what appeals to others.

Thankfully, there's variety and diversity all around us. We should embrace and appreciate those people who have different styles, approaches, and points of view. After all, maybe the person you think is spending their extra money on something silly thinks *you're* the one putting horseradish on your ice cream.

Tyler and Lily, who lived on the west coast, came to me to help them get their finances in order. One day, Tyler used some extra money he'd saved to buy a vintage car with plans to restore it. This purchase was technically outside of his Financial Vision Statement and not consistent with his financial plan, but he had some extra money that allowed him to make this spontaneous decision.

Tyler, along with his friend, bought a 1967 Volkswagen van for $5,000. They planned to spend another $5,000 to restore the vehicle. Much to their dismay—but ultimate satisfaction—they ended up spending an additional $25,000 to completely restore the Volkswagen to a vintage surfer van.

I looked through the pictures Tyler sent me and it's clear that the van is in perfect condition. It brought back many wonderful memories of my youth, surfing in California, as one of my buddies had a van just like it. Anyone who sees this van on the road will be able to tell it was a labor of love and nostalgia.

Although the ultimate cost for this impulse purchase was $30,000 (much more than they anticipated), it's been a great addition to their family.

Many people might think spending $30,000 to restore a vintage van is excessive. However, it's important to note that this purchase didn't affect his cash flow plans or deter him from his vision. This is an example of someone putting horseradish on their ice cream. I didn't need to agree with the purchase or think it was the best use of Tyler's money, because he saw the value of the project, and it brought enjoyment to his life—without causing undue stress or dissension in his family.

Jeff is a longtime friend of mine. He's also another example of someone who moves to the beat of his own drum.

I've worked and associated with Jeff for more than thirty years and, in that time, I've come to appreciate his absolute honesty and willingness to help other people.

Over the decades, Jeff spent his extra income on the expenses related to all his various hobbies. He bought homes to renovate, motorcycles and ATV's to ride. New cars, boats, fishing equipment, and power tools all found their way into Jeff's possession. Through it all, Jeff would go out of his way to generously share what he acquired with others.

From the outside, Jeff's relentless pursuit of his hobbies may look like he's putting horseradish on his ice cream. Yet these purchases are totally consistent with his lifestyle and the values that are important to him.

Who is to say that people like Tyler or Jeff should be denied the things they enjoy just because it's something other people might find unnecessary?

Some financial gurus speak as if we should never use our money to enjoy ourselves. They make others feel that any penny spent outside of their retirement plan, or anything that differs from the guru's personal opinion, is a waste.

I don't believe we can make those decisions for anyone. Tyler and Jeff enjoy the good life. They are responsible with their money and spend their money on things they enjoy.

Food for Thought

Think of three friends or acquaintances that put "horseradish on their ice cream." List what it is they spend money on that you think is different, unnecessary, or frivolous.

Friend 1: ______________________________

Friend 2: ______________________________

Friend 3: ______________________________

Now it's time to look at your own horseradish. List three things you spend your money on that others may think is different, unnecessary, or frivolous.

1. ______________________________

2. ______________________________

3. ______________________________

Example:

Friend 1: My friend accumulates timeshares. He has three weeks every year from three different timeshare companies. I don't think it's a smart investment.

Friend 2: I have a neighbor who leases exotic cars. He looks cool driving around, but he's not building any equity in those cars.

Friend 3: My mother-in-law flies first class wherever she goes, even if the cost is four times more expensive than coach. She could save tens of thousands of dollars every year if she would just fly coach.

Now it's time to examine your own horseradish. List three things you spend your money on that others may view as unnecessary or frivolous.

1. I collect sports memorabilia, and some of the items I acquire are very expensive.
2. I care a lot about my yard so I pay for an expensive landscaping crew to do the work for me once a week.
3. Even though I live in a small house that I'm still paying off, I drive a new Cadillac Escalade SUV.

Our ultimate goal in life should be to become the best version of ourselves—not to become as rich as possible. Money only gives us more of what we have; it doesn't transform us into someone who is more talented, better looking, or more worthy of love.

Rich people have a lot of money. Wealthy people find the balance between earning more, spending less, and enjoying a great quality of life. If you work so hard to earn money that you don't have time to do the things you want to do, you're not free.

As long as your horseradish purchases do not derail your financial plan or put you in financial jeopardy, the details of how you spend your extra money really don't matter. Don't judge yourself harshly for enjoying life as you journey through it.

On the other hand, don't judge others either. We all have our quirks. It's what keeps life interesting.

God says, choose what you will and pay for it.

— Spanish Proverb —

CHAPTER 10

Do or Do Not. There Is No Try

The one with the plan is the one with the power.

— John C. Maxwell —

Throughout the pages of this book, I've shared some of the knowledge and experience I've acquired in the thirty plus years I've worked as a financial coach. I'm hoping you considered the questions I raised and will give careful thought to your Financial Vision Statement. Additionally, I hope you will take a moment to "recognize reality" in your financial situation.

These are only the first steps in a journey that will last your entire life. Financial freedom isn't something you check off a list before moving on to the next project. It's a way of viewing the world and your life experiences. It's learning to have what you want and want what you have.

The truth is anyone can have financial freedom. You can be a millionaire, moderately well-off, or barely getting by. It doesn't matter because once you understand the difference between being rich and being wealthy, once you figure out your financial vision, once you stop comparing yourself to others, once you identify your spending addiction or paranoid saving, you are well on your way to making the personal changes necessary to live financially free.

You may be ready and willing to have financial freedom, yet you're unsure how to travel this road without guidance. In the field of finance, there are many options for people seeking advice and counsel. Some of these options are good, some are great—and some are not good at all. It can be difficult to tell if the person who is offering you a helping hand truly has your best interest in mind. I've developed the EEOCL standard. Before agreeing to work with any financial planner, advisor, coach, or professional, you need to know the answers to these questions.

The EEOCL Standard (Education, Experience, Objectivity, Compensation, and Loyalty)

Questions to ask any financial professional you may potentially work with:

Education:

1. What is your highest level of academic achievement?
2. What is your level of professional education?

Experience:

1. How many years have you been practicing as a financial planner/advisor/coach?
2. Are you willing to share with me some things you've done right, and not-so-right, with your own financial plan?

Objectivity:

1. Do you represent a company or organization?
2. How can I expect you to represent my needs above the needs of the company(s) you represent?

Compensation:

1. Do you receive a commission from any products you're recommending to me?
2. Are you willing to disclose to me what you're compensated on any given product or service?

Loyalty:

1. How long do you plan to be in this business?
2. How do I know that?

There is nothing wrong in working with financial professionals who don't meet the EEOCL standard as long as you understand what is motivating them and can recognize when their objectives are not in line with your objectives.

Why Consider Coaching?

To understand what financial coaching is, let's first look at what the term "coach" means.

Professional athletes rise to the top of their chosen sport because they have a combination of natural talent, learned skill, and incredible work ethic. Also, they have amazing coaches. Olympic athletes, major sports teams, high schools, and local little leagues all need coaches to help them reach their peak performance.

Why is that?

Because when you're working with a competent coach, you're working with someone who is experienced and knowledgeable, someone who can inspire you when needed, point out your weaknesses when necessary, encourage you toward your goals, and keep you focused on doing the best you can.

A financial coach, like myself, is no different than any other type of coach. I work closely with my clients, motivating them, pointing out possible pitfalls, and keeping them focused on reaching their financial objectives.

Just as a talented basketball player can only go so far shooting hoops in their driveway, there's only so much a person can do managing their financial situation on their own. Just as that same young person joins the basketball team to increase their skill level through practice, hard work, and good coaching, you can go further, accomplishing your objectives faster because you have a coach to work with you.

As a financial coach, one of the best parts of my work is the opportunity to assist people over the course of their lives.

Sarah was referred to me thirty-one years ago. When we first met, we looked over her very disorganized finances and put them in order. I helped her see where she was financially strong and pointed out what she could do better. We set up a plan that helped her prepare for retirement. Consistent with her plan, she was able to retire from her job in the public sector. When she retired at sixty years old, she told me how much she'd enjoyed working with me. In fact, we still have quarterly sessions, even though she's fully retired.

"I wasn't sure about financial coaching at first," she said. "But you're one of the few people in my life that stayed and really cared about me."

Her words reminded me of the saying, "People don't care how much you know until they know how much you care."

I believe that everyone deserves caring professionals in their lives, whether it's an accountant, attorney, family doctor, or financial coach.

I met Robert in 1975 when we were both in the Air Force ROTC program. We formed a friendship, along with our spouses, and kept in touch even after he went to pilot training, and I moved on to missile launch officer training.

When I began financial coaching in 1982, Robert was still on active duty in the Air Force. When he transitioned to flying for a major airline in 1986, he retained me as his financial coach.

Over the years, I've assisted and coached Robert and his wife, Lynne. They embraced my financial coaching model, and now they're not only rich, they're wealthy and living a great life.

I'm committed to helping Robert and Lynne for the long-term. I have no plans to retire, even though I could do so today. To me, coaching is a lifelong commitment. I plan on working with Robert's family for as long as I possibly can.

Starting Where You Are

A journey of a thousand miles begins with a single step.

Everyone currently has a net worth, a cash flow, and a financial vision (though they may not have written it down). So the first step in your journey to financial freedom is to recognize where you are, then identify your strengths and weaknesses (which we all have).

From there, you can begin to make logical, rational, and visionary objectives on what financial direction you want to take and at what pace.

To do this right, get a financial coach involved from the beginning.

Meeting With a Financial Coach

There are a lot of financial salesmen in the marketplace who want to know all your financial facts so they can figure out what to sell you. To get started, I don't need to know any of that because I'm willing to work with you regardless of your financial situation. All I need to know is that you're serious about becoming financially secure, independent, and free. I offer all potential clients a free consultation so we can decide together if you're ready to take your life to the next level or if you're satisfied with being satisfied.

If that young person in their driveway, tossing basketballs into a hoop, has no interest in improving their game, then they have no need of a coach. Along the same lines, until you believe your current situation needs improving, you have no need for a financial coach.

I'm compensated the same way attorneys or accountants are. After the initial free consultation, clients retain me for my time in sessions. I don't make any commission from anyone, and my costs are always upfront and clear. After all, clarity is one of the most important parts of any good financial plan.

Sessions typically last for fifty minutes, during which time we review your current financial status, compare it to your plan, and assess how things are progressing. During the session, I explain financial principles particular to your financial situation. We discuss what needs to be addressed, and I give appropriate recommendations. Then we talk about anything else that you feel needs to be addressed at that time. At the conclusion of each session, you will always have at least a few items to take care of before our next session.

Thank you for reading my book. I'm interested in you and would love to be of service where I can.

The best investment you will ever make is in yourself.

— Anonymous —

ABOUT THE AUTHOR

Greg Kesten has spent more than thirty years in the financial coaching field with a focus on educating and teaching.

His formal education includes a B.A. in Communications from Brigham Young University and an M.Ed. in Guidance and Counseling from South Dakota State University. Greg worked as an adjunct faculty instructor at the University of Phoenix and at Salt Lake Community College teaching finance, business communication, and public speaking courses. Greg served in the U.S. Air Force as a Missile Launch Officer. He also taught leadership development skills for seventeen years to Air Force Reserve personnel, including workshops on financial communication and planning. As a husband, father, and grandfather, Greg is involved in family-oriented issues in the community, and enjoys volunteering with a variety of charitable organizations.

FINANCIAL COACHING

Recently a well known weight loss company began airing television commercials advertising that they now offer personal coaching for their clients' success. Founded over fifty years ago, this company finally came to the determination that real success in health management is enhanced with a personal relationship. Just as coaching is helpful to maintain physical health, it is also helpful in maintaining financial well-being.

I've spent over thirty years coaching people to reach their financial objectives. Visit www.financialfreedom.co (not .com) and subscribe to my free Planning Points newsletter. I know financial coaching can make a difference in your life. In fact, it can make all the difference in your financial future. After you have looked at my website, send me an email. I would love to hear what you have to say.

Financial FREEDOM

Finding What Works for You

For any questions, comments, or further contact please refer to my website.

www.financialfreedom.co

(If you think this is a typo and go to .com,
Robert Kiyosaki will thank you.
If you go to .co, I will thank you!)

FAVORITE QUOTES

VISION

Gratitude is the sign of noble souls.

—Aesop

We all live under the same sky,
but we don't all have the same horizon.

—Conrad Adenauer

Those who have a "why" to live,
can bear with almost any "how."

—Victor Frankl

By changing my beliefs, I change who I am.

—James Allen

At the age of 18, I made up my mind
to never have another bad day in my life.
I dove into an endless sea of gratitude
from which I have never emerged.

—Dr. Patch Adams

A moment's insight is sometimes worth
a life's experience.

—Oliver Wendall Holmes, Sr.

Change the way you look at something,
and the thing you look at changes in response.

—ANONYMOUS

Try not to become a man of success,
but rather try to become a man of value.

—ALBERT EINSTEIN

We see through our beliefs, not our eyes.

—ANONYMOUS

To come to be you must have a vision of being,
a purpose, a principle.
You will become what your vision is.

—PETER ZARLENGA

Having great luck and fortune
is not the conduit to a loving and enjoyable life;
gratitude is.

—LAURA SCHLESINGER

He who gains time gains everything.

—BENJAMIN DISRAELI

Riches are not an end of life,
but an instrument of life.

—HENRY WARD BEECHER

The day you stop racing is the day you win the race.

—BOB MARLEY

The workday starts the night before.

—JEFFREY GITOMER

PLANNING

When it comes to changing our lives, our energy is often better spent in the setting of the sail, than in rowing the boat.

—Dean Byrd

The system you are using is perfectly designed to obtain the results you are getting.

—W. Edwards Deming

However beautiful the strategy, you should occasionally look at the results.

—Winston Churchill

What we continue to do is what we wish to do.

—Laura Schlesinger

Management works in the system; leadership works on the system.

—Stephen Covey

The secret of all victory lies in the organization of the nonobvious.

—Marcus Aurelius

Give me six hours to chop down a tree and I will spend the first four hours sharpening the axe.

—Abraham Lincoln

It takes as much energy to wish as it does to plan.

—Eleanor Roosevelt

When parents are not afraid to give their children a clear, objective and age-appropriate picture of the family's finances, the two generations are more likely to become allies rather than adversaries.

—Olivia Mellan

The significant problems we face cannot be solved at the same level of thinking we were at when we created them.

—Albert Einstein

Systems have a greater impact on behavior than mission statements.

—Andy Stanley

Worry is a prayer for what we don't want.

—John Assaraf

If you are prepared, and you know what it takes, it's not a risk. You just have to figure out how to get there. There is always a way to get there.

—Mark Cuban

Your life: are you riding a roller coaster and having a blast or are you riding a merry-go-round and being safe.

—Larry Winget

Money is a good servant, but a bad master.

—Sir Frances Bacon

Prosperity is living easily and happily in the real world whether you have money or not.

—Jerry Gillies

Being the richest man in the cemetery doesn't matter to me. Going to bed at night saying we've done something wonderful, that's what matters to me.

—Steve Jobs

You can be rich by having more than you need, or by needing less than you have.

—Jim Mott

The point of living is to believe the best is yet to come.

—Peter Ustinov

ACTION

A system is simply a way of getting things done. Systems are habits that you do daily order weekly. They are the mechanics of leadership, and over time, they dictate the extent of our effectiveness.

—John C. Maxwell

In life you begin to get where you are going even before you know where you are.

—Anonymous

The secret of getting ahead is getting started.

—Mark Twain

A journey of a thousand miles begins with a single step.

—LAO-TZU

The man on top of the mountain didn't fall there.

—VINCE LOMBARDI

The most difficult thing is the decision to act.
The rest is merely tenacity.

—AMELIA EARHART

Life is like a bicycle.
To keep your balance, you must keep moving.

—ALBERT EINSTEIN

We make a living by what we get.
We make a life by what we give.

—WINSTON CHURCHILL

Everyone can be great,
because everyone can serve.

—DR. MARTIN LUTHER KING, JR.

In any moment of decision,
the best thing you can do is the right thing,
the next best thing is the wrong thing,
and the worst thing you can do is nothing.

—THEODORE ROOSEVELT.

Money doesn't make you happy,
but the way you manage your money
can make you happy.

—JEAN CHASKY

Money is the opposite of the weather.
Nobody talks about it
but everybody does something about it.

—Rebecca Johnson

Successful people are successful because they form the habits of doing that failures don't like to do.

—Albert Gray

Be where you are otherwise you'll miss your life.

—Buddha

Brick walls are there to stop people
who don't want it bad enough.

—Randy Pausch

The only person you should try to be better than is the person you were yesterday.

—Anonymous

HUMOR

To make 1 million dollars, start with $900,000.

—Morten Shuman

I have enough money to last me the rest of my life, unless I buy something.

—Jackie Mason

I put a dollar in one of those change machines.
Nothing changed.

—George Carlin

I owe everyone, I have nothing,
and the rest I give to the poor.

—Sam Levin

A bargain is something you can't use
at a price you can't resist.

—Franklin Jones

You should always live within your income,
even if you have to borrow to do so.

—Josh Billings

Age is an issue of mind over matter.
If you don't mind, it doesn't matter.

—Mark Twain

What is more important, our money or our lives?
The story is told of Jack Benny
walking down the street one day.
He was held up by a robber with a gun.
The robber said to him,
"Give me your money or your life."
Jack Benny stood there, and the robber, threatening
him with the gun, said again,
"Give me your money or your life."
Jack Benny replied, "I'm thinking, I'm thinking."